Mary
Cassatt

By Nancy Mowll Mathews

RIZZOLI ART SERIES
Series Editor: Norma Broude

Mary
Cassatt
(1844–1926)

1. *Self-Portrait.* c.1880. Watercolor on paper, 13 x 9⅝". National Portrait Gallery, Smithsonian Institution, Washington, D.C./Art Resource, New York

CONTRARY to the popular image of Mary Cassatt (fig. 1) as an isolated phenomenon—a woman who overcame insuperable obstacles to become an artist in a restrictive Victorian era—we now see that she was among many successful women living in one of the most favorable periods for women artists that we have ever known. The conditions for success were right: the age of Impressionism was unusually welcoming to women artists, and her career also coincided with the rise of women's rights activism. Cassatt rose to the top of her field because of her unique talents and circumstances. She participated in a style that continues to grow in popularity, and, along with Berthe Morisot, is one of the few women artists from this period still known to us. But less well recorded by history are the scores of other accomplished women who were her friends and contemporaries and who also achieved prominence in the arts, including Elizabeth Gardner, Louise Abbema, Emily Sartain, Sarah Sears, and others. Far from being an anomaly, Cassatt was at the crest of the giant wave of women who were making their mark on the arts in the Western world in the late nineteenth and early twentieth centuries.

This is not to say that Cassatt and her colleagues did not have to struggle against discrimination—because surely they did—but simply that conditions were better for women in the arts in the nineteenth century than is commonly believed, and in some ways they were better than they are today. The women of Cassatt's generation were tremendously helped by the eruption of the women's movement in the 1840s, which, combined with the current cultural vogue of Romanticism, made women's concerns of general interest in art and literature. Cassatt grew up in Philadelphia reading Jane Austen, Elizabeth Barrett Browning, and George Sand and looking at paintings by Angelica Kauffmann, Elisabeth Vigée-Lebrun, and Rosa Bonheur. She saw that women (and even children) portrayed in contemplative poses in romantic settings were popular themes in art at the time and hardly cared that she was barred from drawing nude male models in her art classes. When she was sixteen she entered the Pennsylvania Academy of the Fine Arts in Philadelphia, just as the Civil War was beginning, and found that the war had siphoned off many of the male students, leaving more spaces and attention for the women. By the time she was ready for further training in Europe, her fundamental goals had been shaped: steeped in the Romanticism of her youth, she wanted to become the great interpreter of the theme of the contemplative woman, and she intended to paint "better than the Old Masters."[1]

Europe in the second half of the nineteenth century offered American artists a valued place in society and a freedom they did not have at home. This was especially true for women for whom escaping the velvet bonds of convention in Philadelphia or Boston was a heady experience. Although for the most part young women like Cassatt conducted themselves with as much propriety as they would have at home on Chestnut Street, they luxuriated in the freedom to live in their own apartments, to travel around Europe according to their own schedules, and in general to feel that their professional training was putting them in command of their destinies. Most American artists and art students, including Thomas Eakins and Cecilia Beaux, returned home after three or four years, but others, such as Whistler and Cassatt, grew to view this freedom as essential. They and many other Americans like them, both men and women, made homes for themselves in England, France, or Italy; while participating in the cosmopolitan art circles of Europe, they also served as hosts for traveling American friends and acquaintances in search of some small measure of this freedom—no matter how temporary—for themselves. Thus they kept one foot on each side of the Atlantic and eventually reaped the benefit of having an international audience for their art.

For about ten years (1865–1875) Cassatt moved restlessly around Europe as she visited museums, studied with popular teachers, or worked on her own in picturesque villages. She was inspired to paint folk traditions and costumes, such as carnival scenes and bullfighters, and she hired models who appeared exotic to an American eye. To create a romantic mood, she posed her models to suggest flirtation from a balcony or the melancholy of a lost love (fig. 2). She borrowed the dark, rich colors and chiaroscuro of sixteenth- and seventeenth-century art and created monumental figures in the traditional academic style (plate 1). It was an ambitious art—monumental in subject matter and scale—and soon drew the attention of the juries of the Paris Salon, where she exhibited almost every year from 1868 to 1876.

2. *A Mandolin Player*. 1868. Oil on canvas,
36¼ x 29". ©Philadelphia Museum of Art.
Private collection

Cassatt learned, however, that even in Europe one paid
a price for freedom. While she painted in Italy, Spain, and
Belgium and sent finished works to the Salon, she, in effect,
thumbed her nose at the notoriously cutthroat Paris art world.
But soon she saw that her chances of advancing from promis-
ing art student to famous artist were rapidly dwindling; she
had to succeed in Paris or not at all. Thus, in 1875, she took
up permanent residence there and faced all the challenges
of an overgrown yet still powerful art establishment. She
might have joined fellow American Elizabeth Gardner,
who went to Paris and gradually climbed the ladder to
academic success. Or she might have followed the path
of Louise Abbema, a popular Salon painter who would be
portraitist to the political and artistic stars of her day, including Sarah Bernhardt. Instead, after struggling unsuc-
cessfully to find a middle ground between her own willful
ideas and the polish demanded by Salon juries, she was
suddenly offered another alternative: the anti-establishment
style of Impressionism.

In 1877 when Degas invited her to forego submitting to
the annual Salon in favor of exhibiting with the group that
had been dubbed "Impressionists," it was a sign that she
was well known enough in Paris to have been noticed by
a group of artists who were essentially strangers to her. She
may have encountered Berthe Morisot during the time they
were both copying at the Louvre (1860s), and she may have
known Alfred Sisley and his wife; but Degas himself was
unknown to her before he came to her studio with his invitation. Although she may not have been formally introduced
to the artists, she certainly knew their art, which had been
exhibited as a group in 1874, 1876, and 1877 and could
be seen at various dealers in Paris. Degas's art, particularly,
had already impressed her, and she had begun to make some
small changes in her own work to experiment with the style
that was lighter and more contemporary in mood than her
own. As she considered Degas's invitation, she thought
grimly of what it would take to achieve success in the offi-
cial arena, and she knew that whenever possible she would
always choose freedom.[2]

Although she had to abandon the dark, melancholy
Romanticism of her work for the past ten years, she found
she could easily make the transition to the Impressionist
aesthetic because at its center was her favorite theme: the
contemplative woman. At home, in the garden, in a café,

or in the theater, the heroic modern woman was shown by
the Impressionists as undisturbed by her surroundings,
with lips calm, eyes averted, and keeping her own counsel.
It was a style that gave dignity and respect to women as
well as to many of their universal means of expressing
themselves: their homes, their gardens, and their fashions.
Furthermore, Impressionism was practiced by women—not
just by the dark, intellectual beauty Berthe Morisot, but by
Marie Bracquemond and Eva Gonzáles, who were among
the many women artists who were also married to artists
in these circles. Even some of the models began to paint,
such as Manet's "Olympia," Victorine Meurent, and Degas's
model Suzanne Valadon.

Cassatt quickly translated a favorite motif of hers,
the balcony scene, into the Impressionist idiom and began
painting theater subjects to show at her first Impressionist
exhibition in 1879 (plate 2). Turning her back to the stage,
Cassatt trained her eyes instead on the young women in the
audience. In her many variations on this theme, she explored
the hidden feelings only slightly betrayed by a hunched
shoulder or an unfurled fan. Some of her women are ob-
servers—others, like those in *The Loge* (plate 3), are stiffly
aware of being observed—but all are depicted in bold ab-
stract shapes or blazing colors, a palette that led critics
to praise this newcomer to the Impressionist group and
led Gauguin to buy one of the theater pastels and make
his heavy-handed comparison of Cassatt to Morisot: *"Miss
Cassatt a autant de charme, mais elle a plus de force"* ("Miss
Cassatt has as much charm, but she has more power").[3]

Cassatt's changeover to Impressionism eliminated many
of the problems that a woman artist had when dealing with
the Paris art establishment. She no longer had to submit her
work to an all-male jury and engage in the kind of political
maneuvering that went on behind the scenes in a system
based on favoritism. Nor did she have to compete in an
arena in which the nude male figure was considered the
greatest subject—barred from mastering this subject she
was thus *a priori* barred from achieving greatness.

But the Impressionist group presented its own obstacles,
not as blatant or as damning, but nevertheless significant.
She found that such an informal group had its own informal
means of exclusion and discrimination, such as the café life
upon which the group depended for its interaction and freedom of expression, but which nevertheless excluded "re-
spectable" women such as Cassatt, Morisot, Gonzáles, and
Bracquemond. These women countered the café culture
with their own "salons" (mostly dinner parties or evening
entertainments), in which intellectual discussions and
plans for upcoming exhibitions would last well into the
night. Cassatt herself lived near the Impressionists' café,
la Nouvelle-Athènes, and passed it every day on her way
to her studio on the Boulevard de Clichy. Although she
could not comfortably enter the smoky, working-class bar,
she would daily encounter Degas, Caillebotte, or George
Moore, who would run out for a word with her and go off
for an extended discussion at her studio or in her well-
chaperoned parlor.

There were other restrictions that a woman painting in
the Impressionist style was subject to. Cassatt did not have
access to the seamy side of Paris that inspired Degas's
scenes of brothels or to the risqué entertainers in the
café-concerts. Nor did she feel comfortable painting in

public as Monet would do at the Gare St. Lazare, or he and the other landscapists would do along the Seine. Furthermore, she also found that some female models, looking for romantic entanglement on the side, did not like to work for women artists, thus reducing her pool of available new faces. These restrictions no doubt had an effect on the range and scope of her work, which tends to show a single monumental figure in the simplest of poses and located in the simplest of settings.

But it is also true that Cassatt's single-mindedness as an artist came from internal predilections and interests as much as from external restrictions, since she could easily have painted the street scenes of Paris from her own apartment window, as Caillebotte and Pissarro did, or hired ballet dancers to pose in her studio, as Degas did—yet she chose not to. Even when compared with the work of other women artists of her day, Cassatt's subjects and stylistic devices are doggedly repetitive, as if she were eternally searching for perfection in the texture of flesh, the silhouette of a sleeve, or the line of the back that would bring her monumental contemplative woman to life. She found her studies endlessly fascinating and felt that slight changes in setting or composition made each work unique.

Like many Impressionist painters, she liked to use the people around her to capture psychological nuances and the heroism of everyday life. In 1880–1881 she turned to her sister Lydia, an elegant woman seven years older than she, as her model for a series of paintings to be shown at the Impressionist exhibition of 1881 (plate 4). Lydia combined a fashionable appearance with an intriguing calm demeanor that was made more profound by the pain she was always struggling to hide. Lydia Cassatt had been in ill health for many years and had recently been diagnosed as having the kidney ailment, Bright's disease, from which she died a year and a half later, in 1882. In such paintings as *Lydia at a Tapestry Loom*, Cassatt studied her sister's transparent complexion and pinched features as she bent over her needlework. Cassatt's exploitation of her sister's appearance and inner pain was done in the name of art rather than for personal feelings, since she sold virtually all these canvases from the exhibition. Other family members who consented to sit for Cassatt always did so at their own peril, because they typically found that the portraits she painted, such as that of her mother's cousin, *Lady at the Tea Table* (plate 6), were praised as works of art but were not flattering as likenesses. Although Cassatt did not leap from subject to subject, as did Degas, whose subjects included jockeys, dancers, and nudes, she exercised her own brand of daring—confronting pain and bare reality head on and turning them into art.

Cassatt bristled at challenges to her art of any kind, whether they came from offhand remarks by one or other of her friends or from a confrontation with great art of another culture or era. She was always measuring her own art against the art of others, and, although humble in her appreciation of others' accomplishments, she would often adapt certain devices into her own work to see if she could master them or improve on them. Such is the case of a suite of color prints she designed and carried out in 1890–1891 (plates 8 and 9). These ten prints, done "in imitation of the Japanese,"[4] were a direct response to a vast exhibition of Japanese woodblock prints from Paris collections that was mounted

at the Ecole des Beaux-Arts in 1890. She visited the exhibition with the critic Philippe Burty, who pointed to the superimposition of line and color and said, "No European could do that." Cassatt, "with true American grit," set about to prove him wrong.[5] Cassatt spent the next year working on the designs and mastering the multiplate process for color printing; once the plates were cut in drypoint and aquatint, she inked each plate by hand and worked side by side with a printer to complete an edition of twenty-five impressions for each image. The combination of color and linear design she achieved by this time-consuming process was extraordinary and would become influential in the growing color-print movement of the 1890s.

Her goal was to unveil the set in the annual exhibition of the Société des Peintres-Gravures, and she was furious when the society made a new rule banning all non-French artists from the show. As a result the dealer Paul Durand-Ruel, in whose gallery the exhibition would be held, offered her an adjacent room all to herself, and she was able to give the prints a proper launching. However, she paid for her temper and her sensitivity to challenges when, at the opening of the joint exhibition, the group teased her unmercifully for her attention-grabbing tactics, and she left stunned and almost in tears.[6] Cassatt chose the "narrow and hard" path,[7] which occasionally exacted a high personal toll, but in the end she felt it was worth it. The set of color prints lifted her art to new heights and is now considered one of the great achievements in nineteenth-century printmaking.

By the time Cassatt began working on the color prints, she had already developed a new version of the contemplative woman: the mother with her child. This subject was popular among both male and female artists in the Symbolist climate of the late 1880s because of its layers of psychological and spiritual meaning. Cassatt, who had never abandoned her determination to paint better than the Old Masters, poured all her intensity into the modernizing of one of the grand themes of art. The discipline of investigation that she had learned from the Impressionist style stood her in good stead because her mothers and children are as calm and matter of fact as her women at the theater or in the garden. In the many years that she returned again and again to the subject (from 1888 to 1914), she varied the mood from the intensely solemn, as in *The Bath* (plate 10), to the lightly decorative, as in *Patty-Cake* (plate 12), but she seldom resorted to the type of emotional cliché that has made the work of other maternal genre specialists such as Eugène Carrière or Gari Melchers lose its appeal.

Cassatt's mother and child paintings grew out of a social and political climate in which people were searching for new truths to replace dying Western institutions. Cassatt was of the generation that saw the Crimean War, the American Civil War, and the Franco-Prussian War follow in quick succession; she witnessed the changes in human social habits that were brought about by the railroads (then automobiles and airplanes), electricity, and the telephone. Her brother Alexander J. Cassatt (who became president of the Pennsylvania Railroad in 1899) was a modern tycoon, controlling more lives and resources than the president of the United States. She herself was a modern woman: educated, independent, and working alongside men to reach an audience on two continents. Cassatt's mothers and children are solemn in the face of these challenges to old traditions, but

3. *"Modern Woman"* decoration of South Tympanum. 1892–1893. Oil on canvas, 12 x 58".
Art and Handicraft in the Women's Building of the World's Columbian Exposition,
Chicago. Chicago Historical Society

offer to conservatives and progressives alike the reassurance that love and security are still to be had in the nurturing and protective gestures of one human being to the other. In the hands of other artists, the mother and child theme may have been used to preach the gospel of domesticity in the face of women's entry into the modern world, but for Cassatt it was the glorification of the strong and capable woman in her most ancient guise, as can be seen in *Maternal Kiss* (fig. 4).

In 1892 Cassatt was offered the commission for one of two large murals that would decorate the Women's Building of the 1893 Chicago World's Fair (fig. 3). Cassatt's mural was to show "Modern Woman" in opposition to the mural "Primitive Woman," which would face it across the vast hall and show at a glance the progress women have made over the centuries. Cassatt might have taken this opportunity to show a triumphant goddess with the attributes of railroads, electricity, and other technical advances around her or she might have shown women at work in the many professions they had entered by the 1890s and which were lauded in a series of lectures that took place throughout the fair. But instead Cassatt chose a theme that was to her the epitome of modernism: women plucking fruit from the Tree of Knowledge. As with her maternal pictures, the color and design were light-filled and brilliant, but the figures themselves were solemn and contemplative. As they picked the fruit of Knowledge, they handed it down to other women as well as to young girls, forming an unbroken female chain. The mural was a tribute to women's education, in which there had been major advancements, especially on the secondary and college levels, during her lifetime. The mural was also a celebration of her own personal thirst for knowledge that was carried out every day in her studio, brush in hand. But at the same time it was a call to responsibility in that a woman who had plucked the fruits of Knowledge faced expulsion from the safety of her Victorian Eden and would need to chart a new course in unexplored and often hostile territory. The fact that other women were also taking the journey was comforting, but in the end, each would have to face her own personal challenges alone.

Cassatt cared about conveying this message to the next generation of women, and after 1900 there is an increased emphasis on the children in her mother and child paintings. Often both the mother and an older child are nurturing an infant seated in the mother's lap. And, in a series of paintings and pastels that were unprecedented in her earlier work, she shows young girls assuming the poses and fashionable garb that she had previously used for adult women (plate 13). These girls already have the inward calm and contemplative mien of their older sisters, giving them extraordinary presence despite their age. As Cassatt grew older, she spent

more time counseling the young, whether they were American art students trying to find their way around the Paris art world or her own nieces and nephews. She in turn became a legendary figure, sought out in her Paris apartment or in her country house by those bold enough to face the peppery old woman who would lecture them on the value of hard work.

Cassatt lived long enough to see the ratification of women's suffrage in 1920, a cause that had brought her out of her private feminism into her one act of political radicalism. This was her participation in a joint exhibition with Degas (with a selection of Old Masters) that was organized in New York in 1915 by a friend of hers, Louisine Havemeyer. Havemeyer had amassed one of the finest art collections in the United States with Cassatt's help and used it to further the cause of women's suffrage with benefit exhibitions throughout the 1910s. Cassatt was gratified that her exhibition was successful but outraged that her own family, which had gone over into the anti-suffrage camp, had boycotted it. She took this as a lack of appreciation for her art and her ideas and was renewed in her belief that she could not have accomplished what she did if she had stayed at home in the bosom of her family. Even in her seventies,

4. *Maternal Kiss.* 1897. Pastel on paper, 22 x 18¼". ©Philadelphia Museum of Art. Bequest of Anne Hinchman

when her American friends and family urged her to come home to escape World War I, which was literally fought in her backyard, she would not consent to reenter that stifling atmosphere. "After all give me France," she had once written to a friend. "Women do not have to fight for recognition here, if they do serious work."[8]

When Cassatt died in 1926 she was still considered by many to be America's leading woman artist, even though she had not painted in more than twelve years. But she herself acknowledged that her success was due not only to her own efforts, but to the support and opportunities that were opened up for her by others, many of whom were women. She counted among them her mother, who brought her to Europe as a young art student when her father refused to encourage her; her companion/maid, Mathilde Valet, who ran her household for over forty years and nursed her in her old age; Sarah Hallowell, the American art curator and organizer who brought her to the attention of the organizers of the Chicago World's Fair; Bertha Palmer, the president of the Board of Lady Managers of the Women's Building, who boldly gave the "Modern Woman" mural commission to the progressive Cassatt; and Louisine Havemeyer, the collector and feminist organizer, who was also Cassatt's best friend for fifty years. These and many others—artists, writers, sisters-in-law, and nieces, as well as dressmakers and servants, formed the support system that allowed Cassatt to work on such a high professional level. If she chose the contemplative woman as her lifelong theme, it was not only in celebration of her own choices, but in tribute to the heroic women around her.

NOTES

1. "[Cassatt] laughed when I told her your message and said she wanted to paint *better* than the old masters." Eliza Haldeman to her mother, May 15, 1867. Archives of the Pennsylvania Academy of the Fine Arts, Philadelphia.
2. Achille Segard, *Mary Cassatt: Un Peintre des Enfants et des Mères* (Paris: Ollendorf, 1913), p. 8.
3. Segard, p. 63.
4. In the catalogue for "*Exposition de Tableaux, Pastels et Gravures par Mlle Mary Cassatt,*" (Paris: Galeries Durand-Ruel, April 1891), Cassatt interjects the comment "*Essai d' Imitation de l'Estampe Japonaise*" after the first entry, *Bain d'Enfant.*
5. Grace Gassette, "Mary Cassatt, Painter and Etcher," in *The Art Review*, 17, no. 3 (December 1908), p. 31.
6. Segard, p. 87.
7. "'There are two ways for a painter,' she [Cassatt] has often said to me, 'the broad and easy one or the narrow and hard one.'" Louisine Havemeyer, "Address delivered by Mrs. H. O. Havemeyer at Loan Exhibition, Tuesday, April 6th, 1915," (p. 2). Pamphlet issued in conjunction with exhibition, "Suffrage Loan Exhibition of Old Masters and Works by Edgar Degas and Mary Cassatt," M. Knoedler, April 7–24, 1915.
8. As quoted in a letter from Sarah Hallowell to Bertha Palmer, February 6, 1894. Archives of the Art Institute of Chicago.

FURTHER READING

Broude, Norma. *Impressionism, A Feminist Reading: The Gendering of Art, Science, and Nature in the Nineteenth Century.* New York: Rizzoli, 1991.

Higonnet, Anne. *Berthe Morisot's Images of Women.* Cambridge, Mass.: Harvard University Press, 1992.

Lindsay, Suzanne G. *Mary Cassatt and Philadelphia.* Philadelphia: Philadelphia Museum of Art, 1985.

Mathews, Nancy M. *Cassatt and Her Circle: Selected Letters.* New York: Abbeville, 1984.

——————. *Mary Cassatt.* New York: Abrams, 1987.

—————— and Barbara Shapiro. *Mary Cassatt: The Color Prints.* New York: Abrams, 1989.

——————. *Mary Cassatt: A Life.* New York: Villard, 1993.

Weitzenhoffer, Frances. *The Havemeyers: Impressionism Comes to America.* New York: Abrams, 1986.

First published in 1992 in the United States of America by Rizzoli International Publications, Inc.
300 Park Avenue South
New York, New York 10010

Copyright ©1992 by Rizzoli International Publications, Inc.
Text copyright ©1992 by Nancy Mowll Mathews

Library of Congress Cataloging-in-Publication Data

Mathews, Nancy Mowll.
Mary Cassatt/by Nancy Mathews.
    p. cm.-(Rizzoli art series)
        Includes bibliographical references.
        ISBN 0-8478-1611-7
        1. Cassatt, Mary, 1844–1926—Criticism and
        interpretation.
I. Cassatt, Mary, 1844–1926. II. Title. III. Series
ND237.C3M27 1992   92-15548
759.13—dc20   CIP

Series Editor: Norma Broude

Series designed by José Conde and Betty Lew/Rizzoli

Printed in Singapore

Front cover: See colorplate 7

Index to Colorplates

1. *Head of a Young Girl.* c.1876. Cassatt believed that "some of us are born into the world with . . . a passion for line and color" (letter to Bertha Palmer, October 11, 1892). Even before she learned the Impressionist style and theory, she showed her love of the pure ingredients of art in studies such as this.

2. *At the Theater.* c.1879. Cassatt's experiments with subtle psychological nuances make her work difficult to interpret. In this case, the woman leans forward, engaged in what she is watching, and yet her face is in deep shadow as if she is simultaneously pulling away. In contrast to her beautiful "female" attributes—hair, dress, and bust—her face appears almost ghoulish with its odd pattern of light and dark contrasts.

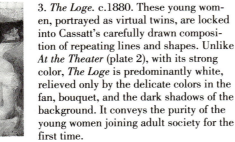

3. *The Loge.* c.1880. These young women, portrayed as virtual twins, are locked into Cassatt's carefully drawn composition of repeating lines and shapes. Unlike *At the Theater* (plate 2), with its strong color, *The Loge* is predominantly white, relieved only by the delicate colors in the fan, bouquet, and the dark shadows of the background. It conveys the purity of the young women joining adult society for the first time.

4. *Lydia at a Tapestry Loom.* c.1881. Little is known about Lydia Cassatt (1837–1882), Mary's oldest sibling. She was well-educated and well-read, but, unlike Mary, was happy in a domestic role. She would at times run the households of her brothers before their marriages and was her sister's chaperon and companion in Paris during the mid-1870s.

5. *Susan on a Balcony Holding a Dog.* c.1882. When Cassatt's parents and sister came to live with her in Paris, they settled in a fifth-floor apartment on the Avenue Trudaine, only a few blocks from her studio on the Boulevard Clichy. This view from their window looking up to Montmartre is one of the few views of Paris to be found in Cassatt's paintings.

6. *Lady at the Tea Table.* 1883. In the mid-1880s the Cassatts saw a great deal of their cousins, Mary Dickinson Riddle, her daughter Annie Riddle Scott, and the Scott children. Mrs. Riddle had been considered a great beauty in Pittsburgh in her youth and was not pleased to see Cassatt's exacting depiction of her aging face; she did not accept the portrait even though Cassatt had done it as a token of friendship and gratitude.

7. *Young Woman Sewing in a Garden.* c.1883–1886. Cassatt's study of Japanese prints dates back to her earliest days in Paris. In her paintings, she occasionally used the extremely stylized devices associated with woodcut prints, such as a flattening of space and a strong diagonal axis. The model in white sits quietly absorbed in her sewing—the calm center in the midst of a background of forceful design and strong color.

8. *The Letter.* 1890–1891. Cassatt's series of ten color prints paralleled the Japanese book or portfolio of prints, which shows an unfolding of daily events, seasons, or types of people. In Cassatt's prints the same models appear in several images, such as *The Letter* and *In the Omnibus* (plate 9), giving us the impression we are following an identifiable woman through her daily routine in Paris.

9. *In the Omnibus.* 1890–1891. The omnibus was the principal mode of transportation around Paris and was ridden freely by women in the course of their daily activities. Cassatt originally had intended to depict it more accurately—as more crowded—but decided against the extra figures that are included in her initial drawing for the print. In addition to this change, Cassatt altered the design six more times while working on the three plates needed to print the final colored version.

10. *The Bath.* c.1893. Cassatt shows the mother washing her daughter's feet with the same absorption in her downcast eyes as her other models showed in *Young Woman Sewing in a Garden* (plate 7) or *The Letter* (plate 8). The tasks these women are engaged in may seem simple, but they are far from mindless—each woman seems lost in a revery of the highest order.

11. *Summertime.* c.1895. In 1894 Cassatt bought the château Mesnil-Beaufresne, located in the small village of Mesnil-Théribus fifty miles northwest of Paris. Some of the first paintings she did there were of the large pond behind the house where she kept a boat for fishing and feeding the ducks. Perhaps because of her delight in her new country home, these boating pictures are looser in handling and are among her most successful outdoor scenes.

12. *Patty-Cake.* c.1897. The fine pastel technique Cassatt developed in the late 1890s was partly the result of her study of the eighteenth-century pastels of Maurice Quentin de la Tour, which hung in the museum of St. Quentin. She later established a scholarship for American art students but stipulated that they spend a year in St. Quentin studying the great pastelists of the previous century.

13. *Simone in a White Bonnet.* 1901. When Cassatt found a child who modeled well, she invariably did a number of studies such as this. The off-center design and clasped hands are devices she had used frequently over the years for her adult models (see plate 2), and used in this context they give the child a strong presence.

1. *Head of a Young Girl*. c.1876. Oil on panel, 12¾ x 9."
Museum of Fine Arts, Boston. Gift of Walter Gay

2. *At the Theater.* c.1879. Pastel on paper, 21¹³/₁₆ x 18⅛".
The Nelson-Atkins Museum of Art, Kansas City, Missouri. Anonymous Gift

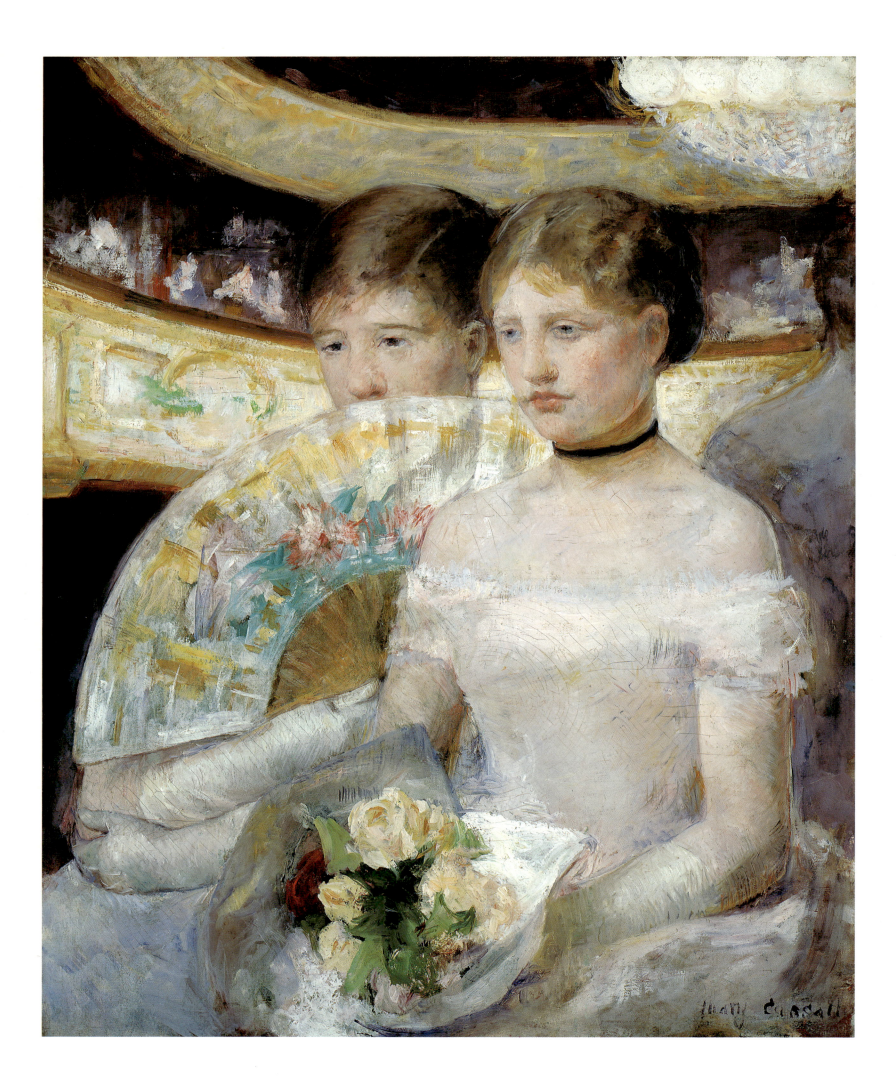

3. *The Loge*. c.1880. Oil on canvas, 31½ x 25⅛".
National Gallery of Art, Washington, D.C. Chester Dale Collection

4. Lydia at a Tapestry Loom. c.1881. Oil on canvas, 25¾ x 36¼".
Flint Institute of Arts. Gift of The Whiting Foundation

5. *Susan on a Balcony Holding a Dog.* c.1882. Oil on canvas, 39½ x 25½".
The Corcoran Gallery of Art, Washington, D.C. Museum Purchase, Gallery Fund

6. *Lady at the Tea Table.* 1883. Oil on canvas, 29 x 24".
©The Metropolitan Museum of Art, New York. Gift of the artist, 1923

7. *Young Woman Sewing in a Garden.* c.1883–1886. Oil on canvas, 36 x 25¹/₂".
Musée d'Orsay, Paris. Photograph ©Réunion des Musées Nationaux

8. *The Letter*. 1890–1891. Drypoint, soft-ground etching, and aquatint in color, 13¹¹/₁₆ x 9".
National Gallery of Art, Washington, D.C. Chester Dale Collection

9. *In the Omnibus*. 1890–1891. Drypoint with aquatint on paper, 14⅝ x 10½".
©The Metropolitan Museum of Art, New York. Gift of Paul J. Sachs, 1917

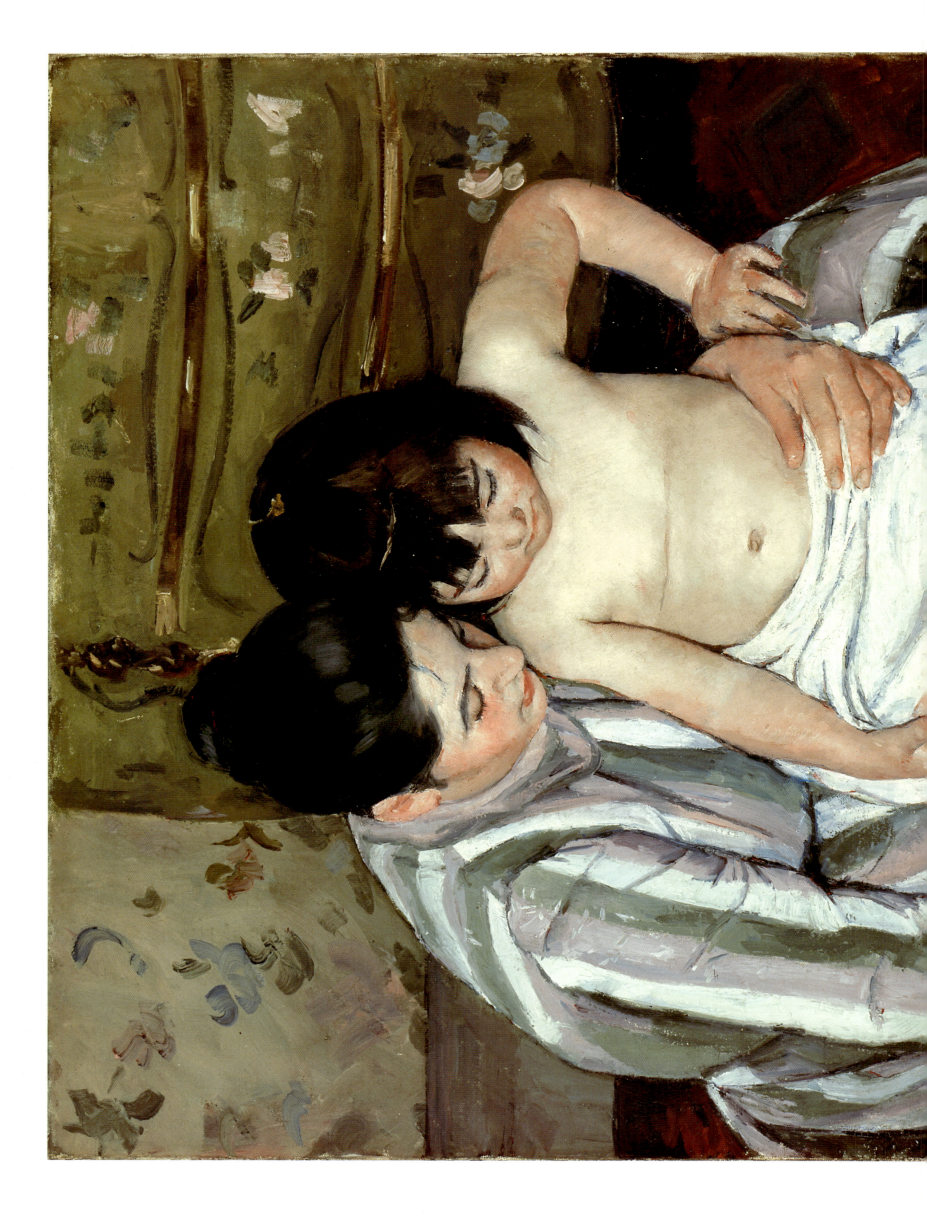

10. *The Bath*. c.1893. Oil on canvas, 39¹/₂ x 26".
The Art Institute of Chicago, Robert A. Waller Fund, 1910.2.
Photograph ©1992, The Art Institute of Chicago. All Rights Reserved

11. *Summertime*. c.1895. Oil on canvas, 28⅞ x 39⅜". The Armand Hammer Collection, The Armand Hammer Museum of Art and Cultural Center, Los Angeles

12. *Patty-Cake.* c.1897. Pastel on paper, 23 x 28½".
©The Denver Art Museum

13. *Simone in a White Bonnet*. 1901. Pastel on paper, 25$\frac{1}{2}$ x 16$\frac{1}{2}$".
Private collection. Photograph courtesy of the Richard York Gallery, New York